AF647259

Praise for *Magadh*

Magadh. Kashi. Kosambi. Hastinapur. Kapilavastu. Ujjaini. Avanti. Shrikant Verma's *Magadh* is about the great cities of the past, imperial or otherwise, that now exist 'only in name'. Allegorically, *Magadh* is also about present-day metropolises, Delhi most of all. In the 1970s and '80s, as a member of Indira Gandhi's Congress party, Verma knew its political culture at close quarters and played an active role in it. These shimmering cities, with all their corruption, both moral and economic, will go the way of Magadh. They'll cease to shimmer, then cease altogether. 'Horseman, / where does this road go?' Therein lies Verma's tragic vision. Twentieth-century Indian poetry has seldom been translated well, and very rarely as well as Rahul Soni's rendering of this Hindi classic. – ARVIND KRISHNA MEHROTRA

Forty years after, these poems are more relevant than ever, telling of power's hollow victories, the peculiar burden of joy, how sorrow finds us wherever we may hide. This luminous translation renders Verma's classic into timeless English verse. One of its many questions – Whose corpse is this? – has been answered by our own ongoing hollow moment: yours and mine. – JEET THAYIL

Shrikant Verma's *Magadh* defies existing labels, other than that of riveting oxymoron. The slenderest of books that is nonetheless an epic. An epic with neither gods nor villains; an epic that stands as a testimony not to heroism but to the transience of glory, of power, of empires; an epic that, alas, remains more relevant than ever. Rahul Soni translates Verma's chronicle of epochal brokenness – its sonic grandeur, deceptive simplicity, et al – with the austere grace, the quiet assurance of a master calligrapher. This is a book I cannot help returning to, over and over.

– KARTHIKA NAÏR

Shrikant Verma brought to everything he did, whether poetry or journalism, a coruscating insight into the modes and styles of political supremacy. In *Magadh*, his collection of verse, excellently translated, we can see, eerily prefigured, our own present: the grand illusions, the raucous vanity, the chronic self-doubt and ultimate fragility of power. – PANKAJ MISHRA

The poems in Shrikant Verma's *Magadh* remind us that power in the kingdom is always decadent, whatever the name of the kingdom. Words spring from the ruins of cities that rise and fall, and Verma's poems act as interruptions, gadflies, shaking us into altered states. Rahul Soni's translations render the original Hindi cadences into English deftly, retaining the philosophical and hypnotic quality of the original, setting up a kind of call and response between poet and reader. In an age where there are significant threats to the republics of our imaginations, Verma returns us to the power of poetry, which is to find 'a third way' – reaching to name that which is not easily named.

– TISHANI DOSHI

One of the best things about reading a good book is that it makes one want to rush out and buy everything else by the writer. It makes us hungry for more. On that count, *Magadh* and its translation by Rahul Soni scores high ... When one first encounters Verma's pointedly sparse poems, the impact is electric. His unfussiness forces the mind to focus on the cacti of dilemmas and questions that never quite leave ... Reclaiming *Magadh* for a new generation of Indian readers was necessary and Soni's translations go a long way to enable this. He communicates both the wiry frame and the lean flesh of these poems for readers in English.

– ANNIE ZAIDI, *DNA*

A reality that is growing more and more monstrous every day and an insensitive politics that stands lost and speechless before this worsening social scenario: these poems try to go beyond these polarities. There is no ready-made solution, nor a well-made philosophy here; it just raises some ethical questions from the battlefield of the present ... Rahul Soni has spared no efforts to capture the deceptive simplicity, the odd rhythm, the quaint irony and the informality that mark the style of the original.

– K. SATCHIDANANDAN, *Frontline*

Rahul Soni's unshowy and often deliberately unidiomatic renderings ... are not the first English translations of these poems, but they are the best in print. [They] closely mimic the short, spent lines of Verma's Hindi and capture their recurring contrasts and paradoxes, their air of dejection.

– NAKUL KRISHNA, *The Oxonian Review*

[I]mpeccable. Soni's immersion in the text has resulted in a pared down, burnished rendition of Verma's cycle of poems. His care with line breaks, his use of words chosen not just for meaning but sound, argue for a kind of rigour that is very welcome. Soni's note on the translation is a gem of precision and clarity...

– SRIDALA SWAMI, *The Sunday Guardian*

Rahul Soni's translation, sharp as freshly cut paper, reserved in temper like old leaves, does the seemingly impossible: it carries two things intact – a sense of the original Hindi idiom and the claustrophobic political culture of the times.

– SUMANA ROY, *Open*

SHRIKANT VERMA

MAGADH

TRANSLATED FROM THE HINDI BY RAHUL SONI

eka

eka

First published in English as *Magadh* in 2013 by *Almost Island*

Published in English as *Magadh* in 2023 by Eka, an imprint of Westland Books, a division of Nasadiya Technologies Private Limited.

No. 269/2B, First Floor, 'Irai Arul', Vimalraj Street, Nethaji Nagar, Alapakkam Main Road, Maduravoyal, Chennai 600095

Westland, the Westland logo, Eka and the Eka logo are the trademarks of Nasadiya Technologies Private Limited, or its affiliates.

Original copyright © Shrikant Verma Trust, 2023
Translation copyright © Rahul Soni, 2013, 2023

ISBN: 9789395767750

10 9 8 7 6 5 4 3 2 1

All rights reserved

Typeset by Jojy Philip, New Delhi 110 015
Printed at Manipal Technologies Limited, Manipal

No part of this book may be reproduced, or stored in a retrieval system, or transmitted in any form or by any means, electronic, mechanical, photocopying, recording, or otherwise, without express written permission of the publisher.

For Nirmal Verma

CONTENTS

FOREWORD

APOORVANAND

Magadh by Shrikant Verma is an iconic poem in Hindi literature. It took time for its significance to be recognised by readers. It was received with bafflement by critics when it first appeared, and their response was largely ambivalent. It could have been mainly to do with the personality of the poet himself. As it happens, his reputation came between the poem and the readers.

The readers found it difficult to reconcile the fact of the poet being an integral part of the power apparatus with a poem which seemed to talk about the futility of the claims of power. Shrikant Verma was a leading figure of the then-ruling Congress party. He, in his own words, was the person responsible for designing the campaigns which persuaded the people to put the party in power even after ousting it twice. He was the general secretary of the party and a member of the Rajya Sabha. So, he was a seeker of power, one who used his creative energy to perpetuate it. When such a person creates a work like *Magadh*, readers react to it with disbelief. That is what the living presence of the creator does to its creation.

But as time passed, the poem started growing on readers. I call it a poem even though critics have read it as a series of poems. It can be read both ways. In my opinion, it is a long poem weaving together different episodes in a sequence, carrying the theme of the ultimate futility of power and also of the final truth of mortality.

The title of the poem created a lot of confusion in the minds of readers. The titles of different episodes, like Magadh, Kosambi, Kapilavastu, Takshashila, Pataliputra, Kashi, Ujjaini, Vasantasena, created the illusion of a historical narrative. But the poet himself has made it clear that the Magadh of this poem is not the Magadh of history: 'this is not the Magadh you've read about in books,' he cautions his readers.

These are poetic devices to help the poet conjure an enchanted world. In an interview, he explains that, from the very beginning, he had wanted to take his readers into an enchanted state, to put them under a spell. To do that, he travels back into history and cultural memory. With all the names, he knits a mystical veil, behind which lurks the contemporary, the present time.

All these names then turn into metaphors. It is not a coincidence that nearly all these names are in some way associated with Ashoka and Buddhism. Shrikant Verma was heavily influenced by them. In an essay written for his party conference after the publication of this poem, he rues that, while there are hundreds of Kalingas, there is no one like Ashoka to say, 'Futile was Kalinga.'

What is the central theme of *Magadh*? The poet told an interviewer that it was 'kaal', an Indian concept difficult to translate into English. One translation could be 'time'. But the poet feels that the closest to 'kaal' is 'death'. He agrees with the painter Sayed Haider Raza who, while reading *Magadh*, wrote to the poet and critic Ashok Vajpeyi: 'Shrikant Verma has written about something which is not and will probably never be.' What could that possibly be? Is the poet looking for a Magadh where people could be true, autonomous beings and where power would never be able to colonise the imagination of individuals?

Magadh talks about the conflict between the desire for power and the search for meaning. It is also about the loneliness of the individual. The references embedded in Indian history and mythology can mislead the reader into believing that the poem is located in India and is about India. But Shrikant Verma is essentially a poet of world sensibility. He has a deep sense of being a resident of the world. He was a keen reader of world literature and a keen observer of world politics. He saw the cruelty behind the claims of the so-called free world of establishing democracy, and also the hollowness of the promise of revolutions. As can be seen in *Magadh*, Verma is concerned with the question of violence, which power of any kind cannot avoid.

Magadh is essentially a poem in search of ways to realise the potential of democracy. Can we cultivate and evolve a democratic sensibility in the true sense of the term? Or is it bound to fail? This is not an Indian predicament alone, the world knows after losing nearly a century in the search for a true, democratic way of life.

Rahul Soni has performed the very difficult feat of rendering the poem into English. The simplicity of the poem is deceptive, because Hindi readers have often felt that you can sense what it wants to say and yet have not been able to fully articulate that. Soni knows the power of that prosaic simplicity and has been faithful to it in his translation. The English literary world will definitely be richer after the publication of this volume.

TRANSLATOR'S NOTE

RAHUL SONI

I first encountered Shrikant Verma's *Magadh* in 2007. A friend had recommended it to me, and I started translating it almost immediately, before I had even finished reading the collection in its entirety.

The first edition of this translation came out in 2013, and it is a curious feeling, revisiting these poems a decade later.

I remember, when I first read them, being struck most of all by the language, which is, I think, still the most arresting thing about the collection – the almost-paradox of its pared-down vocabulary and repetitions, against the slippery circularity and riddle-like ambiguities of its locutions. There was also the intense, often unbearably overwhelming, even indiscriminate, sense of loss – for times, for places, for people – that haunted its pages. I had never translated anything until then; in fact, I didn't think of what I had begun doing as 'translation' at all – I was just so struck by the voice of these poems that I wanted to see if it was possible to achieve those effects in the language I wrote in, i.e., English.

But in these ten years, I have seen these poems become more and more relevant and urgent, speaking with what might seem like remarkable prescience and precision about our current political moment. Except that they were actually a response to a similar moment almost fifty years ago. (Although they are also, like any great work of art, much more than just a response to any particular moment in time.) I also discovered, in the interim, that the language employed here and the feeling that suffuses these poems are something of an anomaly even in Verma's oeuvre. Which gives one an idea of how immediate and visceral these poems must have been when they were first written (some in 1979, and the bulk of them in 1984) and when they were first published in Hindi. These are no mere abstractions.

And now the wheel of history has come full circle – and how quickly, and with no lessons learnt.

The first few poems launch us straight into the world of the book – by and large set around the historical empire of Magadh, during the period (roughly the sixth to the second century BCE) when it grew, under rulers such as Bimbisara, Ajatashatru, Chandragupta and Ashoka, from a powerful kingdom in the eastern part of the Indian subcontinent to one of the greatest empires the world had seen, with Pataliputra, once a minor fortress town, becoming its capital and turning into one of the world's major urban centres.

And then, it all fell into decadence and decline.

> But there is
> neither Magadh nor Magadh
> You too have been searching
> brothers,
> this is not the Magadh
> you've read about
> in books,
> this is the Magadh
> that you
> like me
> have lost

Around it and after it, various other kingdoms (Avanti, Kosal, Videha, etc.), cities (Hastinapur, Kashi, Kosambi, Nalanda, Takshashila, Ujjaini, etc.) and dynasties (the Guptas, the Licchavis, etc.) of antiquity, too, went through their own life cycles, as did religions and schools of thought and art.

These are not just historical places, however – most of them have a rich existence in myth, in classical and religious literature, in the imagination of a people and their culture. The resonances run vast and deep. And one of the most interesting things Verma does is to overlay the historical with the mythic and literary – his allusions range from the Ramayana, the Mahabharata and the puranas to Buddhist texts, from the *Kathasaritsagara* to the plays of Bhasa and Bhavabhuti – magnifying in almost subliminal ways the reach of these poems into the recesses of the readers' psyches.

That being said, I have always held that a knowledge of the cities and kingdoms mentioned in *Magadh* is not necessary for an understanding of the poems. They function more as totems of a sort – a vague idea of them as places and kingdoms that existed once, were once powerful, and are now no more, lie almost forgotten, is what haunts the poems. And I think that a more detailed knowledge – or seeking to understand the poems in terms of specifics with respect to the places and names mentioned – might even distract from getting to what they are trying to say. They are meant to throw a shadow, and perhaps *only* a shadow.

The 'pastness' of *Magadh*, then, at least in my reading of it, is not a pastness that is rooted in the specifics of history, in the details of place or time, but more in the idea of history being cyclical, of the essential nature of things (i.e., people, kingdoms, power) remaining the same, the fact that there are discernible patterns which will repeat themselves, and the weariness, the sense of resignation and futility that such a realisation engenders. (And, indeed, the realisation of the futility of art in the face of this inexorable turning: 'What I wrote, useless / What I did not, / meaningless'.)

If there is a movement within this cyclical pattern of history, perhaps we see it in how the collection itself moves from mourning, to resisting and searching, to some sort of understanding and acceptance. But in the end, we die, what was lost stays lost, and we start all over again having learnt nothing really, forever doomed to repeat ourselves.

The only consolation, if there's any consolation to be had, is that, perhaps, in the larger scheme of things, whatever that may be, none of this matters at all. It is only fitting, then, that the last word in the collection goes to Time:

> I
> am old now
> I write

my name
in chalk
on every blank wall
I come across

The next day I find
someone has rubbed it out
so thoroughly
as if it had never been written

Now when I shout –
Who did this?
I get the answer –
Time

Time, it must be noted, comes up in the very first poem too, in the voice of a vetal – a malevolent spirit that possesses and reanimates corpses.

recognise me?
Vetal –
my deeds
left me hanging
from a diseased branch
of the tree
            of Time

The most famous vetal of all is, of course, the one from the Vikram–Vetal tales – the riddling ghoul hanging off the back of the great king of legend, Vikramaditya, tossing out conundrum after conundrum, and the king who is doomed to repeat the same trek through the cremation grounds over and over.

This is a very potent symbol, and a great voice – inviting yet dangerous, obsequious yet poisonous, sweet yet curdled – to lure the reader into the book and into the ideas of recurrence and futility it circles around. And to me, the form and the language of the poems mirror and are the perfect vehicle for this idea or vision of history.

In my translations, therefore, my attempt has been to retain the rhythms and repetitions of the original without losing its spoken, dialogic quality. To come up with an English that can carry these notes naturally, without sounding antiquated or too contemporary. To mirror its simple, crystalline vocabulary. To find other devices to replace or replicate the effects of the extensive rhyming in the original. To preserve its ambiguities and circularities.

My method, such as it was back then, was to first try and create poems in English out of the words and images of the originals, and then, throughout the process of revision and editing, find my way back, step by step, to the source. This is a process that helped me, I would like to think, approximate what A.K. Ramanujan and David Shulman have called the 'literal force' of the text.

One of the more difficult decisions had to do with Verma's idiosyncratic punctuation. In the end, I decided to retain it for the most part, changing things only when they were too confusing in English. A related problem was that of capitalisation: Hindi doesn't have upper- and lower-case letters, but English does. Here, I have capitalised the first letter wherever, according to my reading, a new sentence begins, whether or not the punctuation indicates it.

The spellings of proper names do not always follow accepted English norms, but are a balance between what might seem natural to a Hindi speaker and what a non-Hindi reader would still be able to recognise or look up.

Some words have been retained from the original, for cultural specificity or where exact equivalents were impossible to find: *maharaj*, for king; *rajasuya*, for a ritual that proclaims a king an emperor; *akshauhini*, for a battle formation consisting of fixed numbers of chariots, cavalry and infantry soldiers; *Mahakaal*, for a name of the god Shiva, referring to his status as the lord of time and death; *ghat*, for a series of steps leading down to a body of water, particularly a holy river, often used for religious rites, some specifically for cremation; *dom*, for a member of an 'untouchable' caste that traditionally worked as scavengers or tended to cremation ghats. *Manikarnika* is the primary cremation ghat in Kashi, on the banks of the river Ganga, and is considered especially sacred. *Ambapali* and *Amrapali* both refer to the famous courtesan of Ujjaini – Verma uses both forms of the name, and I have as well.

Revisiting these translations after all this time revealed a number of instances, big and small, where I had strayed too far – some where I had simply misread, some where I was perhaps too enamoured of a formulation or word choice to let it go, some where knowing more about the context shifted the meaning slightly. I'm glad I had the opportunity to rectify them in this new edition.

In the end, I think it only appropriate to leave readers with Verma's own words about *Magadh*:

> Avanti, Malwa, Ujjaini, Kshipra, Champa, Kashi, Kosambi, Kapilavastu, Kosal, Kalinga, Vaishali, Amrapali, Vasavadatta, Vasantasena, Chandragupta, Bimbisara, Ashoka, Ajatashatru – a procession of characters, of protagonists, of cities, of memories, a crowd that has gathered. That is what my poems are. Their main themes are death, destruction and moral corruption. I know what *Magadh* is – Time beyond time!

INVOCATION

Great benefactor! Sea of virtue! Sea of wisdom!
After many, many years
I've come to your door –

listen my host,
I bring you
stories that span generations
the sorrows of cities, of citizens –

recognise me?
Vetal –
my deeds
left me hanging
from a diseased branch
of the tree
            of Time

Great benefactor! Sea of virtue! Sea of wisdom!
By your grace
I'm born
            a human again

And now I ask you to grant me this
if I cannot give voice to you
then you
            give me voice

(1984)

MAGADH

Listen horseman, where's Magadh?
I've come
from Magadh
I must go to
Magadh

Where
do I turn?
North or south,
east or west?

Here I see Magadh,
here it disappears –

just yesterday
I left Magadh
just yesterday
Magadh's people
told me not to
leave Magadh
I gave my word –
I'd be back
before sunrise

But there is
neither Magadh nor Magadh
You too have been searching
brothers,

this is not the Magadh
you've read about
in books,
this is the Magadh
that you
like me
have lost

(1979)

THE PEOPLE OF MAGADH

The people of Magadh
are sorting the bones of the dead

Which ones are Ashoka's?
And Chandragupta's?
No, no,
these can't be Bimbisara's
they are Ajatashatru's,

the people of Magadh say
and shed
tears

It's natural

those who've seen a man alive
only they
will see him dead
those who haven't seen the living
how can they see the dead?

Just yesterday
the people of Magadh
saw Ashoka
going to Kalinga
returning from Kalinga
Chandragupta riding his horse to Takshashila
Bimbisara
in tears

Ajatashatru
flexing his muscles

The people of Magadh
had seen
and they
can't forget
that they
had seen

those who
can no longer
be found

(1984)

CORPSES IN KASHI

Have you seen Kashi?
Where
corpses come and
corpses go
by the same road.

And what of corpses?
Corpses will come,
corpses will go –

ask then, Whose corpse is this?
Rohitashva's?
No, no,
all corpses can't be Rohitashva

His corpse
you'll recognise from a distance
and if not from a distance, then
from up close –
and if not from up close,
then it
can't be Rohitashva

and even if it is
will it make a difference?

Friends,
you have seen Kashi,

where
corpses come and
corpses go
by the same road.

And this is all you did –
made way
and asked –
Whose corpse is this?

Whoever it was,
whoever it wasn't,
did it make a difference?

(1984)

JUSTICE IN KASHI

The council has been dismissed
Councillors, let's go

What had to happen happened
Why then the long faces?
Why this anxiety?
What are we afraid of?

We did not judge –
merely nodding in agreement is not judgement
We didn't even give it a moment's thought

The debaters debated
what did we do?

What's our fault?
We don't call the council
We don't judge
We come to Kashi
once a year
to say only this
The council is unnecessary
everyone has already been judged
before they are born

(1984)

KOSAMBI

Vasavadatta asks,
What came
before
Kosambi?

Vasavadatta!

Before Kosambi
there was only
Kosambi,

after Kosambi
there is only
Kosambi

In return for
Kosambi
you can get
only Kosambi
Searching for Kosambi
Vasavadatta
has reached
Kosambi

(1979)

HASTINAPUR

Consider
a person
who comes to Hastinapur
and says
No, no, this can't be Hastinapur!

Consider
a person
left all alone –
why should he care when the Mahabharata was fought?

If you can,
consider
Hastinapur,
for which
time and again
a Mahabharata is fought,
and no one cares
except that person
who comes to Hastinapur
and says,
No, no, this can't be Hastinapur!

(1984)

THE CUSTOMS OF HASTINAPUR

I say again
without dharma, there can be nothing –
but no one
listens to me.
It isn't the custom to listen in Hastinapur –

those who hear
are either deaf
or have been appointed
to turn a deaf ear

I say again
without dharma, there can be nothing –
but no one
listens to me

Listen or not then
people of Hastinapur! Beware!
In Hastinapur
your enemy is being raised: Thought –
and remember
these days it spreads like the plague:
Thought.

(1984)

KAPILAVASTU

Days in Kapilavastu make the eyes sore
nights
are drowned in wine and whores

The old, cast out for being old
stop
at the border
and look back at Kapilavastu
with greedy eyes

Young brides sometimes
wake up
startled from their dreams

No one is old in Kapilavastu
there's only
the fear of being old
Being young
means only this
that no one old should be in Kapilavastu

Kapilavastu hasn't been
around
too long

(1979)

KAPILAVASTU CALLING

Maharaj! Let's go back –
this desire to rule over Ujjaini is,
if you ask me,
absurd –

Ujjaini is
Ujjaini no more –
neither is justice served
nor injustice

Just as
Magadh is
Magadh no more –
everyone is well fed
no longer
skin and bone

There is pity in no one
There is shame
in no one
No one thinks,
those who think once
don't think again.

It's the same in Kashi –
in Kashi
they're busy counting corpses
No one
has time for the living,

those who do can't tell
the difference between the living and the dead.

Or take Mithila –
where Videha ruled
till just yesterday
In the same Mithila
now suspicion rules
No one respects dharma –
Vishvamitra, Vasishtha,
no one remains –
Maharaj! Everyone dies
no one is immortal.

If you must go somewhere go to Kapilavastu.
He who goes to Kapilavastu
doesn't come back
He who doesn't go to Kapilavastu
spends his life
calling out Kapilavastu! Kapilavastu!

(1984)

TAKSHASHILA

Soldiers seen in Takshashila
in ones and twos
Who are they looking for
Why do they seem so lost

Why do they go
to the fort
and come back
in ones and twos

bewildered
by the fact
that nothing
remains

except a pile of rubble
that every now and then
shouts
Who
created me

(1979)

UJJAINI

The courtesan
whom Kalidasa loved
filled
Ujjaini
like musk
An auspicious
concurrence
Ujjaini
Kalidasa
musk

sometimes
the stars
are so aligned

Now who comes
looking
asking
Mahakaal himself –
Is this
her city,
she
who was
everywhere
like musk

The courtesan
whom Kalidasa
loved

has she
passed by
this road

Wait, stop,
whose
corpse
is this
floating
by
on
the Kshipra

(1979)

THE ROAD TO UJJAINI

All travellers going to Ujjaini:
this road does not go to Ujjaini
and this same road goes to Ujjaini

Till yesterday I'd show the way
saying
Attention! This road goes to Ujjaini
I show the way today as well
saying
Attention! This road does not go to Ujjaini

Travellers!
The truth is that
every road goes to Ujjaini
and that
no road goes to Ujjaini

Ujjaini
forever looks to the road
Ujjaini
has turned away from roads

Then
where should those going to Ujjaini go?
They should go to Ujjaini
and say,
This is not Ujjaini

because we
did not arrive here on the roads
that go to Ujjaini
or on the roads
that don't go to Ujjaini

(1984)

NAMELESS IN AVANTI

Will it make a difference
if I say
I'm not from Magadh
I'm from Avanti?

Of course it will
you'll be taken to belong to Avanti
you'll have to forget Magadh

And you
will not be able to forget Magadh
you'll live your life
in Avanti
without knowing Avanti

Then you'll say
I'm not from Avanti
I'm from Magadh
and no one will believe you
You'll cry –
'It's true
I'm from Magadh
I'm not from Avanti'
and it will make no difference

No one will believe you are
from Magadh
No one will recognise you
in Avanti

(1984)

FICTION

Sir, hear me out
before you go
The Pataliputra
you and I
are fighting for
is in the eyes of others
a fiction

Do you hear?

For them it's not worth
even a moment's thought
They ask,
What Pataliputra?

Sir! You have to
answer them,
make them understand –
this is the same Pataliputra
for which
Ajatashatru, Bimbisara,
Chandragupta,
you and I
are fighting
Did you tell them?

Sir,
did you hear their retort?
'Fools
fighting for a fiction'

(1984)

SOME OTHER AMARAVATI

Maharaj
this is not that Amaravati
this is some
other Amaravati

No one's ready to fight for it
No one shouts
'I'll give my life
for Amaravati'

No one says
bursting with pride
'Amaravati is mine'

Maharaj
this is not the Amaravati
that till yesterday was yours

Now it is everyone's

The memories
have been erased,
the courtesans,
the stage,
the actors, the actresses
are nowhere to be seen

Maharaj!
Forget that Amaravati was ever yours,
even if it was
no one's ready to fight for it

(1984)

NALANDA

I'm going to Takshashila,
where
are you going?

Nalanda.

No,
this road
doesn't go to Nalanda,
it used to
once,
but not
any more.

The road to
Nalanda
has changed
now this
road will
take you
to Takshashila
not Nalanda.
Do you want to go to Takshashila?

Friends going to Nalanda,
often
it so happens that

the roads
you're shown
don't take you
where
you want to go –
like
Nalanda.

(1984)

WHY NOT MITHILA?

My king, don't be anxious –
anxiety makes the body
feeble,
the soul dull,
the voice weak.
Don't be anxious –

these are not reasons enough:
that in all of Mithila
there's not one poet,
that in the whole republic
there is no sculptor,
that Mithila would be complete
if it had but one singer

My king!
The presence or absence
of singers
makes no difference –

these are the things that matter:
wealth, armies, ministers,
the happiness
of your people.

Yes, Avanti has its
singers, sculptors, poets
but what are they doing?

My king! They say
they're creating Avanti –
that's how
they save themselves

They say the process never ends
Avanti is, Avanti will always be!

My king! I don't
understand –
Why has Mithila never been?
Why can Mithila never be?

(1984)

MATHURA'S LAMENT

Do you hear Mathura's lament?

This is what happens –

when Mathura is no more
Mathura cries
Mathura! Mathura!

Mathura is only one example –
take Avanti.
Listen carefully –

do you hear?
Every now and then
Avanti! Avanti!

It's like I said –
when Mathura is no more
when Avanti is no more
people cry Mathura! Avanti!

Maybe it has become
their habit to cry
when cities turn into memories

But –
Mathura and Avanti
are not memories

and even if they are,
will anyone believe
that Mathura and Avanti
are just memories?

(1984)

VAISHALI 1

There is only one name on the lips
of Vaishali's people –
Amrapali

Amrapali is happy that everyone
knows her
Amrapali is sad that
no one knows her

Those who do know
come to Vaishali
repeating Amrapali, Amrapali
the rest
keep away from Vaishali

People of Vaishali! Amrapali
is just an excuse –
those who know others
will come to Vaishali
chanting Amrapali, Amrapali

Those who don't want to know others –
will slip past Vaishali
saying the reason
is Amrapali

(1984)

VAISHALI 2

We'll last, Vaishali will last
and if we don't?
Vaishali will last.

Vaishali is not a city
it is the memory
of those who came
before us –

of those who said
We'll last, Vaishali will last.
And if we don't?
Vaishali will last.

(1984)

THE REPUBLIC OF KOSAL

Kosal is a republic in my imagination
The people of Kosal are not happy
because Kosal is a republic only in the imagination.

The citizens
gamble all day
those who don't gamble
sleep

The citizens tell stories all day
those who don't tell stories
sleep

The citizens
are peevish all day
those who are not peevish
sleep

The citizens
rejoice
in Kosal's past
those who don't rejoice
sleep

Kosal is a republic in my imagination

(1984)

LACK OF THOUGHT IN KOSAL

Maharaj, congratulations!
Maharaj, victory is yours!
There was no war –
the enemy turned back.

Our preparations, though, were thorough.
A four-akshauhini army,
ten thousand horses,
as many elephants.

No half measures!

Even if there had been a war
the outcome would've been the same.

They had no weapons,
no horses,
no elephants,
how could they have fought?
They were unarmed.

Each one of them was alone
and each one was saying
Everyone is alone.

All the same,
this is your victory!
Congratulations!
The rajasuya is complete
you have become emperor –

only, they've left behind some misgivings
for instance –

Kosal can't last much longer,
there's a lack of thought in Kosal

(1984)

THE STYLE OF KOSAL

Come outside Maharaj, outside
your glory
spreads like
            moonlight
Everyone is happy
No one says
            I have something to say

Something has happened
No one
        says anything
they're all afraid
            If ever they speak
they only say –
I am happy

Maharaj, haven't you wondered
how anyone
            can be happy and
not say a thing?

Anyway, Maharaj's glory
            spreads like moonlight
so where's the need
            to say anything?

But this much I will say
            Those who think
            speak out
and their speaking out
            becomes the style

The sad thing is
that Kosal still
still doesn't
have a style of its own

All the same,
come outside
The crowd
is saying in one voice –
We
are happy!

Maharaj,
as many times
as they tell you
tell them –
'My people!
Stay happy'

(1984)

SHRAVASTI

Those who've left Shravasti
come back –

Mendicants still pass by
repeating
Those who've left
fearing sorrow
will find sorrow

Those who come
find sorrow
Those who go
find sorrow

There's as much sorrow in the rest of Kosal
as there is
in Shravasti

Those who've left Shravasti
come back –
Shravasti wants to say this
but can't

(1979)

THE LICCHAVIS

The Licchavis have gone the Licchavis will come back

There'll be lights in the palaces
bangles will sound
from the inner chambers

there'll be markets
there'll be auctions
there'll be alms
there'll be beggars
there'll be desires
there'll be desirers

Then why are the widows sad?
Why is Vaishali silent?

The truth is that the Licchavis will never come

Even if they do
                they'll only say
We were the Licchavis, we are the Licchavis
and so saying
                they'll pass

The Licchavis are not common
that's why they are the Licchavis

(1979)

VASANTASENA

Vasantasena
is climbing the stairs

You won't understand now
Vasantasena,
you are still young

The stairs never
end
whether of progress
or
regress

of arrival
or
departure
or
fall
or
pride

You won't
understand now
Vasantasena

Neither is
ascent
easy

nor
descent,
the stairs
we ascend
are the stairs
we have
to descend

The stairs are indifferent,

who goes up
who goes down
who goes
up then down
or down then up
how many
have been ascended
how many are left
to descend

they neither count
nor hear

Vasantasena!

(1984)

AMBAPALI

Vaishali sleeps soundly,
only
Ambapali
is awake

It's dark
in some other world
morning
comes
slowly

Stars fall

In Vaishali
people are born
people die

Vaishali sleeps
or
has she died
Ambapali
is frightened
in her dream

Don't be frightened, Ambapali!

(1979)

HORSEMAN

Is a horseman
who goes to Kalinga
the same when he returns?

What do people call him –
victor
        or murderer?
Is he
welcomed by
                courtesans
or
does he drift aimlessly?

What happens?

Horseman,
where does this road go?

(1979)

TRAUMA

A full moon night.
A full moon.
A mirror.

In the mirror
looking just like
the moon
the moon's
reflection.

After resting
for a while
the moon
slowly
moved
out
of
the doorway.

I said,
How
silent it is!
Just then
I saw her
in
the mirror –

before I
could

ask,
Who are you,
she
had
already
disappeared.

Years later
remembering
that day
that
incident
it strikes me –
she was
Padmini!

'That's why,'
I say,
'That's why
we are
both
broken,
the mirror
and
I.'

(1984)

COMING AND GOING

Whenever he went
from Kosal to Magadh
from Magadh to Kosal
everyone asked him
the same question –

Are you going
from Magadh to Kosal
or are you coming
from Kosal to Magadh?

What's the difference,
he would say
and try
to evade the question.

But some
questions
can't be evaded –
especially when
we often pass
through Kosal on the way to Magadh
or through Magadh on the way to Kosal.

It's the most important question of all –
Where are you going?

Who
are you looking for
in Kosal and in Magadh?

And
will Kosal
come first
or Magadh?

The truth is
no one knows why
he keeps coming and going
from Magadh to Kosal
from Kosal to Magadh.

Why does he play out the same scenes
over and over again?

Why
does he shout slogans
for Kosal
when passing through Magadh,
against Magadh
when passing through Kosal?

Why
does he raise
over the crumbling forts of Kosal
the tattered flags
of Magadh?

When no answers
are forthcoming
he too
joins those
who grab passers-by
and ask –

Are you passing
through Kosal
on the way to Magadh
or
through Magadh
on the way to Kosal?

(1984)

QUESTIONS FROM FRIENDS

Friends,
it is meaningless
to say I'm coming back.

The question is: where are you headed?

Friends,
it is pointless
to say I'm moving with the times.

The question is: are the times changing you
or are you
changing the times?

Friends,
it is meaningless
to say I've reached home.

The question is:
where will you go now?

(1984)

SHADOW

Years later I found out
that the one
still with me
was not a shadow

I trampled it
it cried
I called it
it was coy
I scolded it
it wrapped itself
around my legs
I said
Stop following me
it faltered

I took my place
in the council
it sat
by my
side

The council
is gone
the assemblies
have fled
The one still with me
can't be a shadow

(1979)

OFFERING

I could have saved myself
but how could I
Those who save themselves
cannot create

I simmered
then blazed
I began to crack

I could have cried out
but how could I
Those who cry
cannot sustain

It was not self-sacrifice
not resignation
not self-abuse
not castigation
What
was it then

I could have blamed someone
but how could I
Those who blame cannot create

(1979)

DISILLUSIONMENT OF A COURTESAN FROM THE TIME OF THE BUDDHA

With each caress
the breasts quiver

From the navel a fragrance rises

Astride
these thighs
only the mighty
can ride their
horse into the river

In search of unending pleasure come
the general,
the prince.

Women swoon.

Malati,
it won't be the same tomorrow
The breasts
will be filled
with pus,
the thighs
will lie broken
like monuments

You'll only be able
to hear footsteps –

whose?
The general's?
Or the prince's?

The river of pleasure
will have run dry

They'll joke
those who rode their
horse –
you too will laugh.

Fetching a corpse from the river
people leave it
at the ghats
and say –
Here lies Time

No one sees Malati.

With each caress
the breasts
quivered.

Only the mighty
straddled
these thighs.
In search of
unending pleasure
came the prince.

Women
swooned.

The irony
Malati,
you'll always be
Malati.

(1984)

BY THE GRACE OF MAHAKAAL

Half cry, half laugh
they all live in Avanti

by the grace of Mahakaal

Half believe that being incomplete
is as meaningful
as being complete

Half claim that being complete
is as meaningless
as being incomplete

Half are speechless, half debate
they all live in Avanti

by the grace of Mahakaal

Half say that Avanti
is incomplete in
the same way as Kashi,

half say that only
immigrants live
in both cities

They all get trapped in their own argument
they all live in Avanti

They laugh
Kashi's pundits at Avanti's learning
Avanti's people at Kashi's assumptions

by the grace of Mahakaal

(1984)

ROOT

Why are you silent, friends?

What's happened in Magadh?

Has the king died?
Or has the queen given birth to a girl again?

Has war been declared once more?
Have sanctions been imposed once more?

What's happened?
Why are you silent?

Was the antidote useless?
Is there no one left in Magadh?

No one knows
what happens to Magadh sometimes
All will be well yet
no one will say anything
no one will open their mouths
Only Shaktar
who can tell a tree
by its roots
thinks and is terrified

Friends,
whoever thinks
will be terrified

(1984)

WAILING FROM THE INNER CHAMBERS

Why is there wailing from the inner chambers?

Ask,
find out
Maharaj
wants to know –

When
sparks
of happiness
fly all around,

when everyone
thinks
of their own
advancement,

why this sorrow?

When
everyone
says
what happened
was right,

why this repentance?

When
everyone

behaves
themselves,

when
everyone
thinks before
they speak,

why these tirades?

Find out.

(1984)

HE WHO WAS YOUNG

Everyone will return
except he
who was young –
youth does not return.

Even if he does
he won't be the same.

White hair, wrinkles,
senility,
fatigue
He will have become old.

It's natural
for a man to grow old
along the way –
whether the way be easy or hard

Why would anyone want
to be called old?

Why would anyone
count his
white hairs?

Why would anyone
want to be surprised
by the wrinkles on his face?

Why would anyone want
to be told
How quickly a man can grow old –
for example, you!

Why would anyone want
to become
an exemplar of senility, death and fatigue?

Everyone will return
except he
who was young.

(1984)

THE DOM OF MANIKARNIKA

The dom often tells Manikarnika,
Manikarnika
don't be sad,
sadness does not become you
There are burning ghats
where not one corpse arrives
and even if it does,
it isn't bathed
                in the Ganga

What else
can the dom say,
who else
but a dom can stay
alone
at Manikarnika

Manikarnika, don't be sad,
sadness is not
for you
It is for those
who come here
it was for those
they leave behind

Yet they are fortunate
they get to leave
their sadness to you
Manikarnika

Manikarnika
don't be sad,

sadness does not become us

There are doms
whose eyes turn to stone
waiting for corpses
but no corpse arrives –

what else can the dom say?

(1984)

A JUST WAR

How is it possible
for the number of dead to be the same on both sides

How is it possible
for the flag to fall
on both sides
For the widows
on one side
to outnumber
the unwidowed
on the other

How is it possible
for the sorrow in one capital
to equal
the mourning
in the other

That there be repentance
on both sides
That there be dharma
on both sides
That there be shame
on both sides
That both sides
lay down their arms
That both be victorious

I say
it is not possible

One-sided the murders
the victory one-sided

One-sided the arrogance
the fear one-sided

One-sided the widows
the unwidowed one-sided

One-sided the sorrow
the mourning one-sided

One-sided the joy
the repentance one-sided

One-sided the dharma
the shame one-sided

The number of dead on both sides
is never the same

(1984)

DESTINATION: CHAMPA

We have to go only to Champa

This road goes only to Champa
Those who have to go elsewhere
should go by other roads
they should not confuse us by asking –
Does this road go to Champa?

Those who have to go to Champa
have no right to ask anything –
Not: where is Champa?
Not: where isn't Champa?
Not: what is Champa?
Not: is it true
that Champa was
and is no more?

We have to go only to Champa

(1984)

PEOPLE GOING TO KANNAUJ

Brothers and sisters, where are you going?
We are all
going to Kannauj,
because everyone
is going to Kannauj

Those going nowhere,
are going to Kannauj
Those going here and there,
are going to Kannauj

Those who love Kannauj
are going to Kannauj,
those who hate Kannauj
are going to Kannauj

Those who know nothing
about Kannauj
are going to Kannauj
Those who know everything
about Kannauj
are going to Kannauj

Who isn't going to Kannauj?

(1984)

THE LAW

I say again, Maharaj –
do not say,
'The law can't be changed.
What applies to others
applies to me as well.'

There are other ways
to confound the council –
the truth is unnecessary
it is unwise
to be prodigal with the truth –

if you must, say
'The law can't be broken,
the law
can be changed.'

Say
'I don't break the law
like everyone
I fear it
But sometimes, citizens,
when it starts to smother
I make
amendments –
the law, after all, can be relaxed.'

(1984)

PATALIPUTRA

A smear of blood upon the forehead
that is the way
coronations are done

Whose blood is it?
Not his,
the star of
Magadh's eye?

Whose
blood is it?
Does
it
matter?
Even a star
can sometimes
pierce
the
eye

The Mauryas don't care
for ill omens
the Mauryas
care
for victory

Between Takshashila and Nalanda
there are
the Mauryas
and there is
the road

The
flag
flutters

It's not
just
the Mauryas
who are
to blame

even earlier
the pundits
had said –

The
night
deepens
in
Pataliputra

(1979)

A YEAR OF POEMS

What I wrote, useless
What I did not,
                    meaningless

(1984)

INTERFERENCE

No one even sneezes
for fear
of disrupting
peace in Magadh,
peace must remain in Magadh
if Magadh
is to remain

If there's Magadh, there's peace

No one even screams
for fear
of disrupting
order in Magadh
Order must remain in Magadh

Where will it be
if not in Magadh?

What will people say?

But what of people?
They even say
that Magadh is now Magadh
only in name

No one even interrupts
for fear
of interruption
becoming the custom in Magadh

Once it starts
interference never stops –

and whatever you do
people of Magadh
you can't escape interference –

if nothing else
a dead body
passing through the city
will interfere, asking –
Why do people die?

(1984)

RELEASE

I want to go to Kashi,
I say
I'm going to Kosal

What's there in Kashi –
there's Manikarnika
corpses come
corpses go

I don't want to go to Kashi

I want to go to Kashi

I say
Unfortunate is he
who goes to Kashi
not Kosal

You've seen Kosal
so come
I'm going to Kosal

There's a difference
between Kosal
and Kashi –
Kosal is not Kashi

I want to die
in Kosal
I say –

Fortunate are they who
find release
in Kashi

(1984)

SHAKTAR

Shaktar! Shaktar!
Shaktar isn't here.
Maybe he's gone towards Takshashila.

Shaktar! Shaktar!
Shaktar isn't here.
Maybe he's returned to Magadh.

Shaktar! Shaktar!
Shaktar isn't in Magadh, or in Takshashila.
You won't find Shaktar anywhere.

Shaktar comes only
when Chandragupta comes.

Shaktar kills
Chandragupta embraces,
sometimes Chandragupta kills
Shaktar lowers his head

Shaktar isn't in Magadh, or in Takshashila.

(1984)

THE THIRD WAY

Voices in Magadh say no rulers remain in Magadh
Those that were there
thanks to liquor, stupidity and laziness
are no longer
worthy
of being called
Magadh's rulers

Voices
in Avanti
in Kosal
in Vidarbha
say the same
There are
no rulers

Those that were there
thanks to liquor, stupidity and laziness
are
no longer
worthy
of being called our rulers
What do we do then?

If there are no rulers
there'll be no law

If there's no law
there'll be no order

If there's no order
there'll be no dharma

If there's no dharma
there'll be no society

If there's no society
there'll be no individual

If there are no individuals
we won't exist

What do we do?

Break the law?

Forget dharma?

Disrupt the order?

Friends,
there are only
two ways:
we can act unethically
and keep
debating ethics

Act immorally
and keep
debating morality

Speak untruth
practise untruth
live untruth –

and keep pretending
to wage wars for truth

In the end
everyone
has to die
but we shouldn't
give our lives
without reason

Friends,
there's also
a third way –

but
it doesn't go
through
Magadh,
Avanti
Kosal
or
Vidarbha.

(1984)

THE ILLUSION

In my youth
if I chanced upon
some old man
leaning on a stick
crossing the road
clutching his heart

I'd pray
for myself,
Lord!
Take me
before I get old

Now I am old
leaning on a stick
crossing the road
clutching my heart

I pray –

Not yet!
Let me at least cross
the road

Listen my fellow traveller,
here,
take
my hand –
help me
across the road

(1984)

PROOF

Leaving their footprints in the sand
they ask, the next day –
Where has the proof
of our travels gone?

Do you know
what answer
they get?

Brothers, go
where
there's no sand

no one can leave
their mark
on sand

(1984)

RETURN

I saw him leave
by this very road:

he was not alone,
there was an army,
elephants,
horses,
chariots,
music –
the works.

And him
in the midst of it all
on horseback
serene
passing by,
as if
he
was in charge,
and the rest
merely
following.

Twenty years later
I see him
return
by this very road:

he is not alone,
there is an army,

elephants,
horses,
chariots,
music –
the works.

And him
in the midst of it all
on horseback
serene
passing by,
as if
someone else
is in charge,
and
he
merely following.

(1984)

ENCOUNTER

Whose reflection do we see in the river
that startles us,
that makes us scream:
No, this can't be true!

But it is true

and we
can only reassure ourselves:
It was an illusion:
this is no river,
this is not the one
the mere sight of whom
can shock us.

We can't
escape the river

It will come to us
in dreams,
it will remind us
You'll be
startled,
you'll scream:
This is the one
escaping from whom
I used to say,
I'm grateful!

(1984)

ROHITASHVA

Whenever you go to Manikarnika
you'll find an old man
huddled in a corner.

Seeing you
something
in his eyes
will light up –

crying
Rohitashva, Rohitashva,
he
will embrace you

Then what will you say?

This, right:
'I'm not Rohitashva
I really
am not
Rohitashva.'

But how
will you convince
the old man
that you
are not Rohitashva?

His hold on you
will get stronger,
he'll exclaim,
'You really are Rohitashva!'

How will you
convince him
whose Rohitashva
is dead
that you
are not Rohitashva?

(1984)

NAME ON THE WALL

When I was a child
I'd write
my name
in chalk
on every blank wall
I came across

The next day I'd find
someone had rubbed it out
so thoroughly
as if it had never been written

Then I'd shout –
Who did this?
I'd get the answer –
Somadatta

I
am old now
I write
my name
in chalk
on every blank wall
I come across

The next day I find
someone has rubbed it out
so thoroughly
as if it had never been written

Now when I shout –
Who did this?
I get the answer –
Time

(1984)

A POETICS OF WITNESS AND COMPLICITY

ASHOK VAJPEYI

In the 1960s, when Hindi poetry was itching for a breakthrough, Shrikant Verma emerged as a poet of anger and anguish, forging a new poetics of interrogation and doubt: a poet who found no comfort in convention or courtesy and who thought poetry should be blunt and hurting if the truths it articulated demanded such bold assertion. His poetry in particular strove to map out in graphic detail the changing geography of a contemporary hell in which both the individual and society were forced to live with a big 'no exit' on the doors.

Coming as he did from a small town, Verma carried within him a deeply lyrical sensibility, which found that the cosmopolitan ethos could only be addressed or coped with through transgression and excess. Later, as a Hindi journalist in Delhi for decades, he was a witness to the many power games played in the national capital. He came to know many political leaders of many ideological hues and colours closely. And then, he became a political leader himself, when he joined the ruling Congress (I) party – first, as a spokesman who brought rare and ready wit to his public communication. From there, he rose to become the General Secretary of the party and, eventually, a Member of Parliament in the Rajya Sabha. It is during this period that he came into an almost daily contact with the hollowness and banality of power. He watched power from close quarters, enjoying a bit of it himself, realising that there were very few ideas or values at play. Power was grabbed, sustained and practised for purely personal gains and greed. To him it became evident that political power had lost all sense of values and was increasingly also devoid of ideas. As a poet he decided to express and explore this shocking, bizarre but 'powerful' reality in his poetry. Magadh, the ancient republic, emerged as a telling and resonant symbol: Verma decided to write a poetry that dealt with the ultimate failure of power both to last and to gain anything abiding and lasting.

The poems in *Magadh* are inspiring in their indictment: they do not try to put the blame for the banality or vacuity of power on any single entity. *Magadh* makes us all complicit with that which eventually drives all power to certain failure, to vainglory. But *Magadh*'s poems also address other themes, such as metaphysical angst and mortality; and the poems peer into the politics of metaphysics as well. Kashi (now known as Varanasi), the ancient holy city, provides itself as a powerful metaphor and is the source of varied images. The classical images in Verma's poetry assume contemporary meanings and resonances. The classical becomes the contemporary.

Our world today is no different from the world *Magadh* so memorably and movingly maps out. Instead of offering false or shallow hope, it forces us to face deep despair. A poetry which enacts the invisible but ever present despair in the world makes us love and change the world. The poetics of witness and complicity triumphs in that it creates the possibility of another or alternative world, another republic of the imagination. The third path, Shrikant Verma said, did exist, but it did not pass through either Avanti or Magadh. His poetry, in a moving way, was and remains the third path away from bipolar power.

SHRIKANT VERMA'S *MAGADH* AND NAYI KAVITA

MANTRA MUKIM

This English translation of Shrikant Verma's 1984 poetry volume, *Magadh*, by Rahul Soni should bring back some necessary attention to a period in Hindi writing known for both its formal experimentation and political vigour. Nayi Kavita (new poetry) in Hindi, beginning well before Indian independence, ushered in an ethic of writing that was highly innovative yet rooted in the everyday, much like *Magadh*. The movement converses with varied historical and literary realities, providing us with a rich context to house Verma's work in.

Born in Bilaspur in 1931, Verma not only became one of the most prominent figures of Nayi Kavita but also played a key role in Indira Gandhi's government during the Emergency – he is said to have coined the infamous slogan 'Garibi Hatao' that in practice became 'Garib Hatao'. His *Magadh* remains one of the most minimal and sparsely written volumes of Hindi poetry. Soni keeps that in mind as he maintains the rhythm and play of the original text, and his translations of Verma's slender, musical verse will be a discovery for readers of Indian and modernist poetry everywhere.

However, Soni's real achievement lies in his ability to creatively interpret each poem before translating it, allowing him to escape a certain literalness and verbosity that feeds into previous translations. A collection like *Magadh* absolutely needed what Ezra Pound might have called 'a second tunnel of translation' – a translation which speaks for itself as much as it does for the original. Soni's English translation, while being attuned to the formal lineaments of *Magadh*, also seems to be sharply aware of the verbal tone and musicality of the Hindi used in the collection.

The circular quality of some of the poems, their shrewd wordplay and an array of historical references makes the collection, otherwise written in everyday Hindi, seem a little distant. Although Verma's language, his diction and syntax, offer no resistance to comprehension whatsoever, it is quite difficult to pin down these poems thematically. The temporal gap between one's literal reading of the poems and an insight into their metaphorical and symbolic significance, if any, is the real challenge of reading *Magadh*. The poem 'Coming and Going' is a case in point:

जब भी वह गुज़रा
कोसल से मगध
मगध से कोसल
आते हुए
हरेक ने उससे यही पूछा –

मगध से कोसल
जा रहे हो
या कोसल से
मगध आ रहे हो?

क्या फ़र्क पड़ेगा,
यह कहकर
उसने
टालना चाहा सवाल को।

मगर कुछ
सवालों को
टाला नहीं जा सकता –
विशेषकर तब जब
अक्सर गुज़रते हों हम
कोसल से होते हुए मगध
मगध से होते हुए कोसल।

सबमें अहम् है यह सवाल
कहाँ जा रहे हो?

कोसल और मगध में
किसे
ढूंढ़ रहे हो?

और यह कि
कोसल
पहले आएगा
या मगध?

Whenever he went
from Kosal to Magadh
from Magadh to Kosal
everyone asked him
the same question –

Are you going
from Magadh to Kosal
or are you coming
from Kosal to Magadh?

What's the difference,
he would say
and try
to evade the question.

But some
questions
can't be evaded –
especially when
we often pass
through Kosal on the way to Magadh
or through Magadh on the way to Kosal.

It's the most important question of all –
Where are you going?

Who
are you looking for
in Kosal and in Magadh?

And
will Kosal
come first
or Magadh?

While the above lines might strike one as a parodist attempt to further the confusion between 'coming' and 'going', which is what it is in a way, it also is a formally playful way to question the stability of certain spaces in history. The two ancient kingdoms of Magadh and Kosal, both of which find an important place in Hindu mythology, are different in their claims to power. While Kosal was the centre of power during the 'Treta Yuga' (the second of the four ages articulated in Hinduism) as described in the Ramayana, Magadh during the 'Dwapara Yuga' (the third age) under Jarasandha (the king of Magadh and an ardent devotee of Shiva) became the authoritarian force in the Indo-Gangetic plains and caused the exodus of various Bhoja tribes to Kosal. Later, the Pandavas travelled from Kosal to Magadh (not the other way round) in order to conquer Jarasandha's kingdom. Thus, the question here of 'coming' and 'going' hints at the larger osmosis of power played throughout history, where the source of one's journey is as much a deciding factor in one's fate as one's destination. In Verma's case, as we'd later see, this walking between ancient Indian kingdoms is painstakingly perpetual.

The frustration all this might hold for some readers is that, overwhelmed by the readability of these poems a touch too soon, they might finish the collection without having been able to properly interpret it. It will be difficult then to have a cumulative sense of these poems. The casual and conversational tone makes the collection only more difficult to interpret. The historical references and their allegorical counterparts, along with the rigmarole of everyday speech, are all part of *Magadh's* poetic landscape. However, these stylistic gestures on Verma's part are not entirely isolated. They come as a part of, and in response to, the specific aesthetic trend of Nayi Kavita.

While conducting a series of video interviews with the critic Rajendra Mishra about the development of Hindi literature in Chhattisgarh, I heard him talk about his encounter with Shrikant Verma in the 1950s, while the latter was still teaching at a high school in Bilaspur. One of the things he remembered was Verma sitting in front of a local laundry centre, reading out poems from journals published around the time. This washing centre in a provincial town of central India, perhaps with a small sitting area in one corner, became the place where Verma acquainted himself with the exciting new changes in Hindi poetry – which he was soon to join after publishing his first collection of verse, *Bhatka Megh* (1957).

By the time he shifted to Delhi, which was in the early 1960s, he was already being recognised as one of the central figures of Nayi Kavita. And if Mishra is to be believed, this geographical and intellectual drift from a small town to the very centre of power is what governs the logic of *Magadh*. According to him, even after being comfortably settled in Delhi for more than two decades, Verma was in a state of crisis while completing this collection. An elected member to the Rajya Sabha, a personal adviser to the Indian prime minister Indira Gandhi during the Emergency and the spokesperson for the Congress party during the time, Verma was visibly successful in politics, and thus it came as a slight surprise to me when Mishra first revealed a certain anxiety, a geographical and cultural alienation, that he saw in Verma and his body of work. The poem 'Nameless in Avanti' can be read in this context, where Avanti possibly symbolises Bilaspur, as Magadh stands in for Delhi:

क्या इससे कुछ फ़र्क पड़ेगा
अगर मैं कहूँ
मैं मगध का नहीं
अवन्ती का हूँ?

अवश्य पड़ेगा
तुम अवन्ती के मान लिए जाओगे
मगध को भुलाना पड़ेगा

और तुम
मगध को भुला नहीं पाओगे
जीवन अवन्ती में बिताओगे
तब भी तुम
अवन्ती को जान नहीं पाओगे

तब तुम दुहराओगे
मैं अवन्ती का नहीं
मगध का हूँ
और कोई नहीं मानेगा
बिलबिलाओगे –
'मैं सच कहता हूँ
मगध का हूँ
मैं अवन्ती का नहीं'
और कोई फ़र्क नहीं पड़ेगा

मगध के
माने नहीं जाओगे
अवन्ती में
पहचाने नहीं जाओगे

Will it make a difference
if I say
I'm not from Magadh
I'm from Avanti?

Of course it will
you'll be taken to belong to Avanti
you'll have to forget Magadh

And you
will not be able to forget Magadh
you'll live your life
in Avanti
without knowing Avanti

Then you'll say
I'm not from Avanti
I'm from Magadh
and no one will believe you
You'll cry –
'It's true
I'm from Magadh
I'm not from Avanti'
and it will make no difference

No one will believe you are
from Magadh
No one will recognise you
in Avanti.

Hindi poetry addressed the issues of postcolonial modernity in a fashion different from Indian English writing or other regional literatures in that it did not have to negotiate the burdens of an inherited colonial language, culture or readership, nor was its scope confined to a particular linguistic state or region. Poetry in modern Hindi was starting to be written as late as in the first decade of the twentieth century. The compositions before that, written in medieval Hindi dialects, were mostly devotional in nature. These compositions, still used in Hindustani classical music, started to appear during the Bhakti period and were used by individual poets and connoisseurs until the end of the nineteenth century. Tulsidas's *Ramcharitmanas*, a sixteenth-century Awadhi adaptation of the Ramayana, is one of the many texts which eventually led to the consolidation of modern Hindi as we know it today.

The process of formalisation arguably began with what is known as the Dwivedi Yuga (the age of Dwivedi), named after the immensely influential writer Mahavir Prasad Dwivedi. Spending most of his literary life towards the cause of modern Hindi, he founded the magazine *Saraswati* in 1900, which for the next seventeen years promoted and published poets with 'modern sensibilities'. These poets, more often than not, subscribed to a glorious vision of India's past and assiduously wrote about its geographical uniqueness and natural splendour. The loci of devotional poetry, Krishna and Radha, were now replaced by a celebratory, yet arbitrary, idea of India and its history. Maithilisharan Gupt's *Bharat-Bharati* (Voice of India) or Shridhar Pathak's *Bharatgeet* (Songs of India) are comprehensive examples of this age. Preceded by writers such as Bhartendu Harishchandra, Dwivedi's contribution lies in his determined effort to establish modern Hindi as a literary language, wedded, in his conception, to patriotism and the nation state.

The contrast between Verma's ideas on ancient India and that of the poets of the Dwivedi Yuga can be easily noted when one looks at how *Magadh* maps a slim and banal landscape of these former kingdoms, and constantly undercuts the stability and harmony that are foundational for a grand narrative. It is also the difference between writers writing before and after Independence. The former, working with no inkling of an independent India and with questions of nationhood looming large, fantasised about an allegorical nation almost as an imperative, while the post-Independence writers, with an eye on communal violence and a certain disillusionment with Nehruvian socialism, challenged the tenets of an erstwhile nationalism in multiple ways. This is how the poem 'Corpses in Kashi', set in a city that prides itself on its ritualistic and sacred qualities, begins:

> तुमने देखी है काशी?
> जहाँ, जिस रास्ते
> जाता है शव –
> उसी रास्ते
> आता है शव!

शवों का क्या!
शव आएंगे,
शव जाएंगे –

पूछो तो, किसका है यह शव?
रोहिताश्व का?
नहीं, नहीं,
हर शव रोहिताश्व नहीं हो सकता

Have you seen Kashi?
Where
corpses come and
corpses go
by the same road

And what of corpses?
Corpses will come,
corpses will go –

ask then, Whose corpse is this?
Rohitashva's?
No, no,
all corpses can't be Rohitashva

However, not all pre-Independence literatures were nationalistic. Chhayavaad, inspired by European Romanticism, tried to bring in humanist elements and personal expression to Hindi poetry. This meant doing away with formal constraints, like rhyming couplets and progression, imposed by earlier movements. Their impact, or rather their context, can be imagined by the notoriety they gained for merely writing blank verse. It is this formal experimentation and freedom that Nayi Kavita owes to Chhayavaad writers. A modern Marxist poet and major practitioner of Nayi Kavita, Gajanan Madhav Muktibodh, published a long study of Jaishankar Prasad's *Kamayani*, one of the masterpieces of Chhayavaad writing, claiming it to be one of his stylistic influences. Nevertheless, Chhayavaad consciously maintained an apolitical stance, often carving its subjects into trans-historical and mythological objects.

This political laxness came in for sharp criticism from Pragativaad (the Progressive movement), which emerged in the 1930s with the formation of the Progressive Writers' Association (1936). Inspired by socialist ideas of revolution and aesthetics, these writers made sure that they wrote in a common idiom and represented a large group of people. Some of the major works of this period, especially poetry, shifted the gaze from an individual 'hero' back to society, and embodied a strict ethics of revolution and change. However, the movement had its own problems as it soon became artistically didactic and ideologically constrained. These issues, too dense to discuss here in detail, are what provoked Nayi Kavita to experiment formally, while at the same time being politically rooted. The poets of Nayi Kavita were not only politically conscious but, like the Pragativaad poets, were also active participants in political change. Thus, when Shrikant Verma, who was at the forefront of party politics for almost a decade, writes 'Lack of Thought in Kosal', it becomes satirical of a kind of politics he himself encountered and was a part of:

महाराज, बधाई हो! महाराज की जय हो!
युद्ध नहीं हुआ –
लौट गए शत्रु।

वैसे हमारी तैयारी पूरी थी!
चार अक्षौहिणी थीं सेनाएं,
दस सहस्त्र अश्व,
लगभग इतने ही हाथी।

कोई कसर न थी!

युद्ध होता भी तो
नतीजा यही होता।

न उनके पास अस्त्र थे,
न अश्व,
न हाथी,
युद्ध हो भी कैसे सकता था?
निहत्थे थे वे।

उनमें से हरेक अकेला था
और हरेक यह कहता था
प्रत्येक अकेला है!

जो भी हो,
जय यह आपकी है!
बधाई हो!
राजसूय पूरा हुआ,
आप चक्रवर्ती हुए –

वे सिर्फ़ कुछ प्रश्न छोड़ गए हैं
जैसे कि यह –

कोसल अधिक दिन नहीं टिक सकता,
कोसल में विचारों की कमी है!

Maharaj, congratulations!
Maharaj, victory is yours!
There was no war –
the enemy turned back.

Our preparations, though, were thorough.
A four-akshauhini army,
ten thousand horses,
as many elephants.

No half measures!

Even if there had been a war
the outcome would've been the same.

They had no weapons,
no horses,
no elephants,
how could they have fought?
They were unarmed.

Each one of them was alone
and each one was saying
Everyone is alone.

All the same,
this is your victory!
Congratulations!
The rajasuya is complete
you have become emperor –

only, they've left behind some misgivings
for instance –

Kosal can't last much longer,
there's a lack of thought in Kosal

The more radical of the modern poets, Muktibodh and Dhoomil, despite their affiliations with progressive values, decided to venture outside the mechanical format of Pragativaad and actively engaged in more creative and individualistic poetics. Lucy Rosenstein, who translated some of the key writers of Nayi Kavita in her anthology *New Poetry in Hindi*, notes how the aesthetics of the movement allowed for, or rather creatively supported, heterogeneous themes and ideas. Unlike other literary movements, Nayi Kavita did not invest its energies into creating a stylistic or political unity. Agyeya, one of the major figures of modern Indian poetry, published a slim anthology known as *Tar Saptak*, which contained one of the first traces of Nayi Kavita. In his introduction to *Tar Saptak*, Agyeya writes:

> They have not reached any destination, they are still travellers – not even travellers, but seekers of a path. There is no ideological unity among them, their opinions on all important subjects ... are different.

Among the poets included in *Tar Saptak* were Marxists like Muktibodh and Freudians like Agyeya himself. It was unique even for Hindi literature to have a movement based purely on artistic affiliations without a unity of ideas or ideology. Shrikant Verma, who does not find a place in Rosenstein's anthology, was one of the several independent voices who came together under the banner of Nayi Kavita. It becomes important then to delineate certain prominent features of this movement in order to theorise its impact on the writing of *Magadh*.

Something that Hindi poetry, even after the subjective strain in the Chhayavaad period, hadn't seen was the focus on the human individual. Nayi Kavita made possible the shift towards a more materialist, yet philosophical, understanding of the human self as a sociocultural being. In Agyeya's own words: 'During the interwar period a ... profound change had been developing. It was purely subjective like Chhayavaad, not merely objective-correlative like Pragativaad, but a basic reorientation towards man. It was a growing awareness ... of the integrity of the human individual.' Although this might seem a little too close to the ideals of Western Modernism, Nayi Kavita's influence must be situated more locally, as a response to the changing industrial-urban conditions of a postcolonial India, the massive violence of Partition, the failure of Nehruvian ideas and, finally, the existent tendencies in Hindi poetry. 'Questions from Friends', one of the few 'personal' poems in *Magadh*, tersely articulates the anxiety shared, perhaps, by millions of people right after Independence:

> मित्रों,
> यह कहना कोई अर्थ नहीं रखता
> कि मैं वापस आ रहा हूँ।

सवाल यह है कि तुम कहाँ जा रहे हो?

मित्रों,
यह कहने का कोई मतलब नहीं
कि मैं समय के साथ चल रहा हूँ।

सवाल यह है कि समय तुम्हें बदल रहा है
या तुम
समय को बदल रहे हो?

मित्रों,
यह कहना कोई अर्थ नहीं रखता,
कि मैं घर आ पहुँचा।

सवाल यह है
इसके बाद कहाँ जाओगे?

Friends,
it is meaningless
to say I'm coming back.

The question is: where are you headed?

Friends,
it is pointless
to say I'm moving with the times.

The question is: are the times changing you
or are you
changing the times?

Friends,
it is meaningless
to say I've reached home.

The question is:
where will you go now?

Rosenstein lists 'the wonderment of everyday life, the ironies of daily existence, communion with nature, musings over philosophical issues, the experience of the creative process, alienation and social inequality' as the major thematic concerns of Nayi Kavita. All the above categories hold equally true for *Magadh*, but not before one wades through the primary complexities of its 'allegorical' narrative. The themes that Rosenstein mentions wouldn't seem necessary at all if one reads the poems merely for their narrative quality. The difficulty of pinning down these poems thematically, as mentioned earlier, is their inviting narrative scheme and their metaphorical subtlety. Thus, poems like 'Destination: Champa' and 'Ujjaini', on the first reading, might just suggest a physical displacement of the places mentioned in their titles. A closer look might also indicate the state of a dispossessed traveller for whom a physical destination has lost all its sociocultural meaning and has probably become a figment of the imagination. One can also read 'Destination: Champa' as symbolising the creative process, as the questions invoked here will prove:

जिन्हें चम्पा जाना है
उन्हें कुछ पूछने का अधिकार नहीं –
न यह कि चम्पा कहाँ है?
न यह कि चम्पा कहाँ नहीं है?
न यह कि क्या चम्पा है?
न यह कि क्या यह सही है
कि चम्पा थी, चम्पा नहीं है?

Those who have to go to Champa
have no right to ask anything –
Not: where is Champa?
Not: where isn't Champa?
Not: what is Champa?
Not: is it true

that Champa was
and is no more?

Sridala Swami, reviewing the translation for *The Sunday Guardian*, talks of how Verma's involvement in national politics and his experience there is 'expressed in often disquieting ways' in some of the poems. To elucidate this point, Swami quotes from the poem 'Interference', where lines like 'peace must remain in Magadh', 'Order must remain in Magadh' and 'What will people say' create a sense of forced harmony and order that is imposed on Magadh, where any kind of interference is to be avoided at all costs. The poem ends by naming death as the ultimate interference, for which Magadh's systematic governance will have no answers. This is where the catastrophic quality of Magadh is laid bare, to be feared and accepted. Verma, who can claim to have an insider's view of power politics, sees annihilation, in this poem and several others, as the only way out of an illusory order. None of the poems effectively restore our faith in any kind of social mobilisation or change, and 'A Year of Poems', quoted here in its entirety of three lines, is a good example:

जो लिखा, व्यर्थ था
जो नहीं लिखा,
अनर्थ था

What I wrote, useless
What I did not,
meaningless

In this case, how does one read *Magadh*, whose understanding of politics is deeply pessimistic, as a statement on the political life of Shrikant Verma? In a piece published in *The Oxonian Review*, Nakul Krishna hints at a kind of expiation that Verma might be looking for through the collection. By 1984, the year when *Magadh* was first published, the true nature and extent of the violence practised during the Emergency years were widely known facts. Verma's complicity as the mouthpiece for the government during these years and possibly an eventual self-realisation is what made *Magadh* appear at the time it did and say the things it said.

However, it would be a mistake to read *Magadh* for merely its autobiographical or confessional elements. A more important area to look at would be the treatment of common citizens who populate these poems. By representing them as dormant figures placed at the receiving end of institutional power, Verma denies them any substantial agency except by virtue of their own passivity. The arbitrary institutions that run these ancient kingdoms of Kashi, Magadh, Kosal and Vaishali amongst others seem to have certain absolute arrangements already in place. While the corpses in Kashi 'come and go by the same road', Kosal's people, in the absence of a republic, are shown to be endlessly rejoicing in their past. Similarly, the greatest fear in 'Amaravati' is that the people do not believe in fighting for their kingdom any more. Although Krishna rightly reads the message in these poems as carrying 'a strong whiff of bad faith', they also extend the scope and theme of the collection, which in its 'Invocation' promises to narrate the sorrows of both cities and citizens.

If *Magadh's* subject matter offers us a labyrinth of political and historical allusions, its form cleanly departs from its content, containing a witty, ironical energy. While some poems in *Magadh* are written in the form of pithy sayings like 'Is a horseman / who goes to Kalinga / the same when he returns?', others appear to be roadside conversations, 'Horseman, / where does this road go?' Nayi Kavita, and its endorsement of free verse and rhythm as multi-layered concepts, has clearly been important in Verma's oeuvre. But *Magadh* is an exception even amongst Verma's other works, none of which achieve the immediacy and terseness of this volume. While Chhayavaad was responsible for bringing out the nuances of poetic form without making use of conventional rhyme and metre, *Magadh* became a landmark work in its exploration of contemporary speech, economised phrasing and extremely innovative use of repetition. The title poem 'Magadh' uses all these three techniques in order to create a gritty sense of desolation and forgetfulness:

सुनो भई घुड़सवार, मगध किधर है
मगध से
आया हूँ
मगध
मुझे जाना है

किधर मुड़ूँ
उत्तर के दक्षिण
या पूर्व के पश्चिम
में?

लो, वह दिखाई पड़ा मगध,
लो, वह अदृश्य –

कल ही तो मगध मैंने
छोड़ा था
कल ही तो कहा था
मगधवासियों ने
मगध मत छोड़ो
मैंने दिया था वचन –
सूर्योदय के पहले
लौट आऊँगा

न मगध है, न मगध
तुम भी तो मगध को ढूँढ़ रहे हो
बंधुओं,
यह वह मगध नहीं
तुमने जिसे पढ़ा है
किताबों में,
यह वह मगध है
जिसे तुम
मेरी तरह गँवा
चुके हो

Listen horseman, where's Magadh?
I've come
from Magadh
I must go to
Magadh

Where
do I turn?
North or south,
east or west?

Here I see Magadh,
here it disappears –

just yesterday
I left Magadh
just yesterday
Magadh's people
told me not to
leave Magadh
I gave my word –
I'd be back
before sunrise

But there is
neither Magadh nor Magadh
You too have been searching
brothers,
this is not the Magadh
you've read about
in books,
this is the Magadh
that you

like me
have lost

Although most of this piece concerned itself with providing a political and literary context for *Magadh* which I thought was necessary, my own reading of these poems has centred largely on the idea of walking in a city and its various configurations. This is not to say that I found the entire collection responding to these themes, but a few sections which actually deal with it were very exciting and enriching for me personally. The ancient kingdoms that we see as titles for many of the poems are not merely, I would think, historical places to hang a narrative around, but fluid spaces which mutate in meaning and form. The poetic persona walks around and towards these spaces, asking for directions ('Horseman'), observing rituals ('The Style of Kosal'), and attributing totemic values ('Return').

These places, which have their mythic significance, are already removed from the poet physically and historically. To describe them in terms of what remains of them for us, like ruins, coins or texts, would only be making them a place for visitation and objective appreciation, unlike the 'walkable' spaces that *Magadh* creates for its narrator. By bending certain rules of logic and cartography, Verma maps a more personalised space of everyday experience, while not making any insistent efforts to make these experiences historically verifiable. Lines like 'Before Kosambi / there was only / Kosambi' and 'After Kosambi / there is only / Kosambi' create a haunting dialectic of transience and permanence. Here, one does not compulsorily need to understand 'Kosambi' as a place where the Buddha lived for two years or as a place created by Brahma's son. Although both these facts enrich our reading, it suffices to see Kosambi as a practice of birth and death, as a world that we walk in and out of.

To walk a city is not see it from a distance as a Euclidian marker on a map, but to make a personal everyday experience out of a given reality. A poem like 'The Road to Ujjaini', which appears as a public announcement, has at its core the uncertainty of a walking experience. More or less, Ujjaini is an idea or feeling which not everyone achieves by taking the same road. The surreal potency of Ujjaini is marked, surprisingly, by the non-teleological characteristics of the road.

उज्जयिनी जाने को इच्छुक यात्रियों से निवेदन है:
यह रास्ता उज्जयिनी को नहीं जाता
और यह कि यही रास्ता उज्जयिनी को जाता है

मैं कल तक रास्ता दिखा रहा था
यह कहकर कि
सावधान! यह रास्ता उज्जयिनी को जाता है
मैं आज भी रास्ता दिखा रहा हूँ
यह कहकर कि
सावधान! यह रास्ता उज्जयिनी को नहीं जाता

यात्रीगण!
सच तो यह है कि
हर रास्ता उज्जयिनी को जाता है
और यह
कि कोई रास्ता उज्जयिनी को नहीं जाता

उज्जयिनी
लगातार रास्ता जोहती है
उज्जयिनी
रास्तों से मुँह फेर चुकी है

तब फिर
जिन्हें उज्जयिनी जाना है, कहाँ जाएँ?
वे उज्जयिनी जाएँ
और कहें
यह उज्जयिनी नहीं
क्योंकि हम
उन रास्तों से नहीं आये

जो उज्जयिनी जाते हैं
या उज्जयिनी नहीं जाते

All travellers going to Ujjaini:
this road does not go to Ujjaini
and this same road goes to Ujjaini

Till yesterday I'd show the way
saying
Attention! This road goes to Ujjaini
I show the way today as well
saying
Attention! This road does not go to Ujjaini

Travellers!
The truth is that
every road goes to Ujjaini
and that
no road goes to Ujjaini

Ujjaini
forever looks to the road
Ujjaini
has turned away from roads

Then
where should those going to Ujjaini go?
They should go to Ujjaini
and say,
This is not Ujjaini
because we
did not arrive here on the roads

that go to Ujjaini
or on the roads
that don't go to Ujjaini

Michel de Certeau, in his famous work *The Practice of Everyday Life*, articulates the walking experience in possibly the most clear and precise terms. He writes:

> Thus the street geometrically defined by urban planning is transformed into a space by walkers. In the same way, an act of reading is the space produced by the practice of a particular place: a written text, i.e., a place constituted by a system of signs.

Even if *Magadh*, due to its allegorical design, does not seem to tackle questions of space directly from the point of view of an individual, it does make an effort to distinguish a place from space. The crux of such an effort lies in its polyvalent approach to places with fixed names and associations. Thus, the person who walks the landscape of *Magadh* receives these places not as they would be meant to be received culturally, but as floating signifiers of various other things, like the birth cycle, urban desperation and totalitarianism. The argument can be extended to Verma's approach to history as well. Far from attempting a traditional historiography in his poems, Verma thinks of history as yet another mirror, which reflects the historian's everyday as much as it is made to reflect the past.

I still wonder how an eclectic bunch of poems such as this, sharing more formally rather than thematically, appeared to me in my first reading as a long sequential poem. The different mythical heartlands that first appear in the table of contents seem to be conjoined by something other than just the immediacy of their medium. Isn't it striking that all these places, which were centres of education and culture in ancient India, appear to us as only relics of the past? Their fall into decadence and an ultimate disappearance is what conjoins them, as they are partially traced in the poems. We see the impending doom in the behaviour of kings (Amaravati) and the populace (Kosal) alike, but what we do not see is the actual point of decimation of these glorious kingdoms. Even walking, an everyday practice, appears to be a circular and tedious exercise, where the people are shorn of any capacity to choose their own destinations. In the poem titled 'People Going to Kannauj', lines such as 'Those going nowhere / are going to Kannauj / Those going here and there / are going to Kannauj' empty any intentionality on the part of the travellers. The rest of the poem is also dedicated to showing us how multitudes of people are walking to Kannauj (and to their fate) without any real purpose or effort. If the cities in *Magadh* are half dead, and this is how they are fated to remain, the process of walking is already doomed. The everyday is caught in its own web of repetition and myopia as the larger world around it faces the challenge of survival. This might be what Arvind Krishna Mehrotra had in mind when he wrote of *Magadh* as containing 'Verma's tragic vision'.

Apart from the names of the cities which repetitively appear in the poems, almost as incantations, the poetic persona at multiple places is seen asking for directions or giving them. One of the key lines – 'Horseman, / where does this road go?' – is telling of the place-oriented approach in some poems. The binary of 'here' and 'there' seems necessary for establishing any kind of personal identity, not only in *Magadh* but also in a world which is sharply divided between the city and the countryside. The geographical assertion, or its need, in the poems explicates the finality of this divide. Verma himself, as we saw earlier with 'Nameless in Avanti', was tackling issues of alienation in Delhi with the view of his small-town upbringing. The dialectics of 'here' and 'there' also extend to the political choices that Verma offers us in his poem 'The Third Way', where the first two options – 'acting unethically while debating ethics' and 'speaking and practising untruth while fighting in the name of truth' – give way to a third one:

मित्रों,
तीसरा रास्ता भी
                    है –

मगर वह
　　मगध,
　　　　अवन्ती
　　　　　　कोसल
　　　　　　या
　　　　　　विदर्भ
　　　　　　　　होकर नहीं
　　　　　　　　　　　जाता।

Friends,
there's also
　　　　a third way –

but
　it doesn't go
　through
　　　　Magadh,
　　　　　　Avanti
　　　　　　　　Kosal
　　　　　　or
　　　　　　　Vidarbha.

The third way, existing in strict negation of the previously available modes, does not affirm any geographical boundary or ethics. It does not even seem to announce its nature or intent. One is not even sure if this third way, presented almost as a chimera here, is achievable in any real terms. This makes it a precarious space within *Magadh*, much of whose solemn geography is limited by history, politics and, in more subtle terms, humanity.

ACKNOWLEDGEMENTS

Everyone, without whose help, comments, suggestions, excitement, support and encouragement, this volume would not exist –

People: Apoorvanand, Sohini Basak, Ashutosh Bhardwaj, Saurabh Garge, Shatarupa Ghoshal, Kanishka Gupta, Giriraj Kiradoo, Arvind Krishna Mehrotra, Sharmistha Mohanty, Mantra Mukim, Karthika Naïr, Vivek Narayanan, Janice Pariat, Arshia Sattar, Minakshi Thakur, Ashok Vajpeyi, Abhishek and Anca Verma, and all the many others who have left their mark on these pages.

Institutions: the British Centre for Literary Translation, the Charles Wallace India Trust, the Jamun, Nrityagram, Sangam House and the University of East Anglia for time and space.

Publications: *Almost Island* and *Asymptote*, where early versions of these poems appeared; Almost Island Books, for the first edition, Westland Books and Eka, for this new one.

Family, friends: for steadfastness, for being there.

– Rahul Soni